THE STORIES II.

ZILINA 2021
JAN KOMOROVSKY

TABLE OF CONTENTS

INTRODUCTION

The Part II. The Nature

Part IV. The Water

INTRODUCTION

This work contains stories that have been collected based on my own experience.

In Part III. The Nature are stories about nature in which we live and which deserves our highest priority attention. The mountains, hills and meadows altogether with waters create a wonderful picture of landscape. Every stay in nature bringing to us peace, relaxation, calm down and lot of energy.

Don't underestimate the mountains and overestimate your strength. Please respect nature, protect our environment and don't pollute it.

In Part IV. The Water, these are stories related water, water which can be once like the sea, sometimes

like a lake or rivers and streams
or well. Water belongs to another
basic elements like earth, fire and
wind or air. Water, it is
greatsource of energy without which
we cannot be.

And an icy crystal clear water
is amazing experience with its
stunning effect.

Part III. The Nature

Winter vacation in a mountain hut

During the winter we liked to go with the children to the mountain hut for the winter holidays to ski during the winter vacation. At that time it was very severe winter, there was a lot of snow everywhere and the weather was sunny.

Upon arrival at the mountain hut, it was necessary to remove a large amount of snow so that I could park our car. The snow was relatively difficult to clear because it was very loose.

The mountain hut was unheated, so I had to heat in the fireplace with wood, the first night we all

slept together in one room to heat
it with an electric heater. But the
next day it was very nice and warm
in the whole cottage.
The children were sledding on a
nearby hill, the sun was very
pleasant and warm. Skiing was just
as amazing in this weather.

Throughout our stay the
weather was beautiful, the blue
sky, no wind was blowing and it was
possible to sunbathe in the sun
because of the weather inversion.
During the day the highest
temperature was only -13°C and at
night it dropped below -20°C of
course we were in very warm
clothes.

We will never forget such a
wonderful time, which only nature
can really create itself.

Open-air museum and storm

If you like history, you will definitely like to visit the open-air museum, where the original houses of the people are located, there are also their farm buildings, manors and often the whole temples have been relocated.

It is mainly a picture of the lives of the people who lived here before us, there are also their original tools, clothes and furniture. It is a very interesting place where you can relax and always to learn something new, because this place is also with a guide. And you can also buy something here, such as various souvenirs, and there is always a good snack in the stalls. In short, we like such places with their unmistakable atmosphere.

Once we went on a trip to the open-air museum, which is a museum of the village and which is located in a mountainous area. After the show, we bought something for refreshments and went on the way back to the place where we parked the car, which was more than three-quarters of an hour from the open-air museum, because we also wanted to walk a bit.

However, we did not count on a change in the weather at all, because there was wonderful summer weather at the beginning of the trip and we did not have any raincoats or umbrellas with us all that remained in the car.

Well, we really soaked in the thread because it was raining heavily, but fortunately there was no storm. Finally we got in the car, inside we changed effortlessly into dry clothes and set off on the way home.

After a few meters, however, the rain seemed to cut and the sun was everywhere. We also laughed at that, because there was rain all around the open-air museum within a few kilometers, but elsewhere the sun was shining.

Open-air museum and steam train

We recently visited another open-air museum, because we were looking forward to riding the steam train, which is liked not only by children but also by adults, who admire the original technique such as steam locomotives.

Steam propulsion is certainly a piece of enormous history, but

also the wisdom and technical
ingenuity of the people before us.

We were very much looking
forward to this trip, because the
track was only recently put into
operation and the section that was
opened was only very short so far.
But we were very satisfied, because
the track led through the forest,
over smaller watercourses and over
meadows. The original buildings of
the station, locomotive depot and
platform are also repaired in the
open-air museum.

We were all satisfied and
people relaxed here, especially by
staying in nature.

Cycling trip. The longest stage

We have planned a summer
vacation together with children in

a recreational area in the north of
our country where we would do not
only alpine tours but also bike
trips.

We were the first to plan a
cycling circuit on our MTBs in the
length of several tens of
kilometers in the foothills and
mountain terrain as a day trip. It
was a circuit first through the
valley, then steeply through a
mountain pass and then slowly down
a very long route to the valley but
another way and back to the
starting point, that is, in the
place of our accommodation.

On the eve of our planned
trip, we prepared clothes, bicycles
in advance and we were looking
forward to the trip together. But
what was our surprise when we woke
up in the morning and the sky was
cloudy. Nevertheless, we got ready,

got on our bikes and set off. But after the first few meters, it was clear that it was not a good choice. After a while, it rained violently and we had to go back. We were happy that the weather has improved and we would go on a trip the next day. But no. The next day we woke up to a cloudy morning. We picked up again and we thought the weather would be better than the previous day, we had traveled a few kilometers but the same thing was repeated as before. Suddenly it rained violently and we had to come back again.

On the third day, we were already quite skeptical about whether we would go on a cycling trip during our vacation at all, whether the weather had stabilized and would be suitable for day

trips. But we were very pleasantly
surprised.

We were greeted by the sunny
weather early in the morning and we
were finally able to set out on our
planned route.

We were really satisfied and
as a reward we got an unforgettable
experience that we still remember.

Cycling trip. Thunderstorm

In my free time I like to do
cycling trips on MTB in my place of
residence as circuits in the
suburbs and in the foothills in the
form of circuits. One of these
circuits is my favorite. This is a
circuit that takes only a few hours
and is therefore suitable during
the working week after my work.

One day I was already looking
forward to riding a bike, because

my work duties had not allowed me to do such an activity for a long time, so I planned this traditional circuit of mine.

I prepared my clothes and a bicycle and set off on a route full of expectations. Everything went very well from the beginning, it was pleasant summer weather, the sun was shining, only a very gentle breeze was blowing and overall the atmosphere was great.

It wasn't until I was halfway there, where this circuit was starting to turn back in the foothills, that a very strong wind suddenly began to rise. At the beginning, I didn't pay much attention to it because in the early evening and in the foothills, it's not unusual.

But to my great surprise, the sky began to change sharply, it was

suddenly black and the wind was
still strong and it was getting
cold. Subconsciously, I started to
accelerate, but we know it won't
help and we won't run away from the
storm. I was already quite close to
where I lived.

Suddenly a very heavy downpour
started, fortunately without a
glacier, but what was worse, it
started to thunder and lightning
struck everywhere. I managed to
hide under the bus stop, but it was
opene and could barely protect me
from the downpour because a very
strong wind was blowing.

But it still thundered and
lightning struck all around. No one
was seen anywhere and the cars
didn't drive either. Of course, I
was worried, because a storm is
always very dangerous mainly in
a open area.

Suddenly, with a deafening
roar, lightning struck very close
to where I was hiding and struck a
nearby tree. At that moment, I was
already scared and just waiting for
the storm to subside. And indeed,
after this blow of thunder, as if
the storm was about to say goodbye,
the thunder stopped and it rained
only heavy but calm rain.

Well, despite the rain, I set
out on my way home, which only took
me a few minutes. I was greeted by
a wife who was really very worried
about me.

Bike trips and racer

In our holiday apartment we
have bicycles that I have prepared
for various cycling trips around
the area, which really provides a
number of different routes.

These routes lead first
through the surrounding villages,
around the fields, then through the
foothills and finally mostly
through the most demanding but also
the most interesting mountain area.

Other routes lead around the
dam, but it is mainly on paved
roads where there are no mountains.
But again, when the weather is
nice, it is possible to stop and
freshenin the water. And then move
on. Entire routes can be planned
either for the whole day or just
for a few hours and there is always
the possibility of refreshments in
the surrounding restaurants.

In short, relaxation and
active rest to recharge your
batteries for further work.

My wife and I once went on a
shorter circuit on bicycles. It was
a beautiful summer morning, the

blue sky, the sun was shining and we were looking forward to this trip. Everywhere we met on the route of tourists either on foot or by bicycle and also together with the children with whom we greeted each other and with some we even talked.

After a while when we were about halfway there we got to a narrow place and I looked to see if anyone was following us. I only saw one cyclist in the back, who was going really fast and it was clear that he was approaching us more and more and he did not slow down or brake at all.

When he was very close to the corner, we were as close to the sidewalk as possible and we tried to avoid it as much as possible. But he didn't slow down at all. He quickly ran around us, almost

catching my wife and after a few
meters he lost his balance and
fell. Fortunately for the bushes.

Suddenly it was very quiet,
the man did not move at all and was
not even visible. I was about to
call emergency medical care. Only
after a long time did we notice a
slight movement, then we saw the
head, later the body and finally
the bicycle.

The man stood up and we will
never forget the look he looked at.
It was a really ugly look. He
didn't say anything as if he were
dumb, he was probably in shock. At
first I thought he would physically
attack me and I was ready for it.
But suddenly something seemed to
stop him when I looked at him.

To break the growing tension,
we asked if it was okay or if we
didn't need to call for help. But

he just replied that he was fine
and didn't need anything.

At that time, my wife remarked
in an innocent voice, "But you're
probably used to such falls."

But it wasn't until a long
time later that he replied, "Yes,
now!"

He had a mountain bike of the
highest available category, which
was obviously brand new. We got on
our bikes and we both went on
without a word.

Well, what else to add. This
really needs no further comment.

Cow

We often went with my wife and
with my children on short trips to
nature for relaxation. At that
time, the children were very small,
barely a few years old.

Once we went to a neighboring
district in nature. It was a
mountain area, cows often grazed
here. We parked the car along the
nearby driveway and went for a
walk. After a while we sat down in
the meadow, the children played
here and we talked.

Suddenly my wife cried out and
I was very frightened. I looked
around and one cow was rushing at
my wife. I didn't think, I took my
backpack and drove my cow with it.
But she was still adamant, and I
didn't want to back down either.
When she saw my determination, she
finally turned around and very
reluctantly joined the other cows.
The children cried a lot, because
it was a big shock. And the same
for my wife.

Of course, I was not aware of
the danger at that moment and I did

not play the brave at all. It was just a simple instinct to avert danger, and I acted impulsively.

Only after a while, when my wife and I could talk about this incident, did we ask each other what could have caused the behavior of this cow, which we still cannot explain.

It was our clothes and its color, our talking, gesturing, maybe it was her territory that she protected. If so, why did she attack only my wife and not me, or the children, for whom it would be really worse.

Horses

For a long time, my wife and I planned a short horseback trip in a nearby mountain area where it has been organized such trips for those who have not yet ridden horses.

Upon arrival, we both did our choice, I chose a horse and my wife chose a mare and after a short briefing, we both mounted and set out on a journey into the woods, accompanied, of course, by our instructor.

Even when I mounted my horse, I was a little nervous and this horse of mine felt it. But after a while I relaxed as my horse felt and suddenly I felt that we were as one whole.

I spoke to him and I really felt like he was communicating with me, he was satisfied but it was also felt that he was a little playful. Our instructor also noticed this and immediately told me not to praise him very much again, because then he is very

capricious. But I didn't pay much
attention to it and sometimes I
spoke to him because it really did
him good. Well, what to add. Isn't
it a bit similar to our people
sometimes?

Bear in the valley

Once in November, because the
weather was exceptionally nice for
this time of year, it was not rainy
at all, the sky was blue and the
sun was shining. We planned a trip
to the valley, which is a very
popular tourist area. There is a
water mill, which is well preserved
and there are the goats and cats.
We parked our car and headed
for the mill, which only takes
three quarters of an hour. But from
the beginning we noticed that there
is no one in the mill except one

tourist with a child. And there was
no one in the mill except the
grazing goats. We walked around the
mill for a while and suddenly we
were left alone in the whole area.

We were about to go back when
we suddenly heard a strange sound.
At first we thought we heard tall
game in the forest but we could
hear the growl, it was the growl of
a bear.

We had to go back in a
completely different way, it's a
detour that lasts about one and a
half hours. In addition to all
this, it was getting dark quickly,
which is usual at this time of
year, and we have already completed
most of our journey in full
darkness. No one was visible in the
area and there was no one in the
surrounding cottages because very
few people go there at this time of

year. In the end, we got to our car
safely and we were happy that it
all turned out so well.

The whole area is a very well-
known locality where many bears
move and there are also many bear
encounters with humans.

Castle

Less than three-quarters of an
hour's drive away is our castle,
which is a very popular place among
tourists.

I used to come here with my
parents and later with my family.
We parked the car on a meadow next
to a mountain stream. At that time,
it was still possible to make a
fire on a small fireplace and
prepare something for grilling or
even to cook goulash together with
friends.

Once we went to this place
with our friends and started
preparing everything here so that
we could cook goulash. My friend
and I cooked goulash, our children
played and the wives rested.

Even when the goulash was
almost finished, an unknown person
suddenly appeared with us. He
talked a lot and it was clear that
he wanted something from us. So we
offered it to beer, but it was
obviously not easy to get rid of
it. In the end, we also offered him
goulash, which he explained by
inviting him to stay there with us.

But we knew that the only way
to get rid of him was to pretend to
leave, which we did, but in the end
we still had to leave because it
was really impossible to shake this
man.

Well, sometimes private entertainment can go wrong in unexpected directions, and we can never know what might happen. However, many often confuse our hospitality with the use of the other.

Mountain hut and sledding

We really liked this mountain hut. It is just over an hour's walk from the car park and is open all year round. It is the starting point for much longer alpine hikes.

One winter we went to this cottage and took a sled so that we could then go down on a sled. The weather was excellent, the sun was shining, the sky was blue and there were a lot of tourists.

After a while, however, the weather changed, a strong wind

began to blow and it snowed heavily. We didn't even see a step. So we stopped in a nearby grove and weathered a snowstorm.

As the storm subsided, we continued on. We rested at the cottage, we dried ourselves, we had a snack and we rested a bit.

The weather had really calmed down and we started sledding down into the valley. The journey down really only took a few minutes. It was an unforgettable experience.

Mountain hut and scooters

One day we went to our favorite mountain hut. The way up takes a little over an hour. It was a wonderful sunny summer time and the weather was excellent.

When we finally got to the mountain hut, we went to see the

nearby waterfall and we also
visited the symbolic cemetery where
there are memories of the victims
of the mountains. New names are
added here every year because the
mountains are really challenging
and sometimes they take their cruel
toll.

On that day we did not
continue on the alpine hike,
instead we rested and sunbathed in
the mountain sun.

We decided to go down on the
scooters that lend here. It was an
amazing experience, we were down in
a few minutes.

Downhill skiing

Skiing is our very popular
activity during the winter. When
you are in good shape, skiing
becomes a truly amazing experience.

Many times you don't even realize
it, but while driving fast, you
feel like if you are floating and
completely forget about moving in
the snow.

Weather permitting, we used
skiing every weekend during the
winter.

We got up a little early in
the morning, got ready, and we were
there in less than a quarter of an
hour's drive. We were in our
favorite winter resort.

We parked the car, put on our
ski boots, bought a ticket and were
among the first to line up for the
lift. It was always better to go in
the morning when there weren't so
many people here.

But the most beautiful thing
was skiing during the spring
months, in March and April, if the
weather allowed. The sun was

already warming and it was always an unforgettable experience. We have already known us in this ski resort, not only the lift staff but also in the restaurant.

But even as skiers, we got to know each other, because there were many people who, like us, always liked to come back.

Declines in youth

I received a notice of a registered item, it was a registered letter, but I did not know who was sending it to me, because the postage note always states only the sending post office and the city, but you do not know the sender's address.

Well, I had to go to our post office to pick up the shipment.

I stood in the crowd and
waited for my turn to come.
Suddenly a woman came up to me:
"Hi, it's you and she addressed me
by name and surname.

I was scared, at first I
thought if she was okay, if she
just didn't want to lure me
somewhere and get money from me, or
if she didn't want to let me know
that she had a baby with me, and so
on.In short, some impostor, which
is nothing new.

But as we started talking,
which, by the way, to my surprise
went very well, she suddenly asked
me, "But you know who I am!" I
simply replied, "Yes, I know." But
after a while, I had even more
doubts, which began to gnaw at me
more and more. But she didn't ask
me anything further, and we
continued our conversation more and

more, which went smoothly and it was clear that we had to know each other for a really long time. That way, I didn't even realize when it was my turn.

When I arranged the necessary matters at the window, we said goodbye. But a shadow of doubt and uncertainty still gnawed at me.

It wasn't until a few days later that I finally remembered. She was my high school classmate!

Part IV. The Water

Beach and sand

We have been preparing for a sea vacation with my wife for a long time and we have chosen a place together. After careful consideration and especially consultation with a representative of the travel agency, which seemed to us to be the best, we chose a place to rest, an island where we planned to spend our moments of relaxation together.

Finally, the date of our departure approached, and with it the traveler's fever and nervousness, but in the end everything turned out very well, arrival by car to the airport, departure by plane, landing and transfer from the airport to the hotel. We were very pleasantly surprised, the place, the hotel and especially the staff with whom we gradually became friends and we were very satisfied with it. We were even so very satisfied that we returned to this place several times over time. In this place we were also introduced to the owners of local shops, where we liked to go shopping for small things and souvenirs.

The beach at the hotel was sandy and had to be reached either by stairs or by a slight detour along the way. But it was a beautiful sight, the scenery was amazing. Right next to the beach was a small cafe and snack restaurant, which was excellent.

Already in the first evening we met a group of women and girls who were here for a reward for a

break as the best sales
representatives of a very well-
known cosmetics company. It was
obvious that they were here alone
and without their partners. We
started talking, but it was clear
that most of them were not
satisfied at all, which led us to a
lot of amazement. Once it was sand,
which bothered a lot, other times
the stairs that needed to come to
the beach or even bothered to walk
around to the beach, by the way,
very comfortably.

Both we are active, during the
day we went to the beach, which was
sandy and which we love very much,
we swam, snorkeled and of course we
sunbathed. In short, the active
rest so necessary to recharge our
batteries for our demanding work,
so that we can continue in it.
Evening walks around the city,

shopping in local shops and sitting
in the restaurant. During our stay
we were several times on a trip to
the capital of the island to see
the historical and cultural
monuments and we were on a round
trip around the island to important
monuments and places.

There were also live music
concerts in this hotel, we could
dance and have fun. In short, we
were very happy with this place of
rest, which we had chosen so well
before.
As for this group of women, we
didn't see them on the beach, they
were usually by the pool, but they
weren't often seen there either.
Maybe they imagined their vacation
completely differently. Otherwise?
But how?

And maybe the reason for their
dissatisfaction was not even what

the beach is, whether it is on it
or not sand, whether it is rocky,
or how far it is from the hotel.

Perhaps the reason for their
dissatisfaction was that they had
no one to share their experiences
and feelings with, which they could
share with their partners and
friends. Who knows?

Beach too far away

We chose a holiday by the sea
on an island in a place that we
really liked, a sandy beach, only a
few tens of meters from the hotel,
a very good hotel and staff. In
short, all priorities.

In the hotel we met a partner
couple who was very nice to us and
with whom we became friends.

Our daily routine is mainly
swimming, snorkeling and of course

sunbathing on the beach. In the morning we always called them to see if they could join us together on the beach, but they always told us with a smile that the beach was too far away, by the way it was only a few tens of meters away, that it was not too clean, and that they would rather relax while swimming pool, where there was also a snack bar. Only once we saw them together on the beach where they were together for a short refreshment by the shore, which made us very happy.

Of course, we did not pay any attention to it, because the way of rest for each person is really his choice and depends mainly on him.

As everything has come to an end, this holiday is over. Later, we sometimes met together from time

to time, because they lived only in
a nearby neighboring district town.

It wasn't until a long time
later that we learned that his
girlfriend couldn't swim because
she had childhood trauma when she
was drowning. We were really very,
very sorry for that.

Rugged beach

Once we chose one place for a
holiday by the sea on an island on
which we were but a completely
different beach. It was actually a
bay that consisted of several
smaller beaches separated from each
other. One beach was completely
sandy, along another beach there
were rocks, another was a rocky
beach, further there was a place
where it was possible to jump from
the rock into the sea. In the

middle of this whole bay was a few
tens of meters away a wide rock in
the shape of a board, on which you
could swim and then climb and rest.
Swimming and snorkeling from one
beach to another was a real
experience in this bay.

In short, it was a scenic view
of this bay. The whole bay was
lined with huge rocks on one side
and amazing beaches on the other.
However, when the wind rose up,
huge waves began to rise here and
swimming was not possible because
of the great danger.

At that time, we chose another
bay, which was only a few minutes
away by taxi or bus from our place.

We were so fascinated by these
places that we spent all our time
just by swimming. It was a truly
unforgettable experience.

Dam and island

In our country there is a very famous artificial reservoir, a dam in the north, which was built more than sixty years ago. Together with the surrounding mountains, it is a very popular recreational area for summer as well as winter sports and for fishermen. The dam wall of this building had to be repaired after some time. The dam was drained and for a short time in the summer, flooded houses and other buildings could be seen. Even in the summer, the inhabitants of the surrounding villages began to grow various crops at the bottom of this artificial reservoir.

After the completion of construction work, they began to

refill the dam with water. Because the entire tank was cleaned, the water was extremely clean and suitable for swimming and water sports. Therefore, we chose a holiday in a cottage near this dam.

The weather during our vacation was really perfect, blue sky all day, no storms, in short ideal weather.

We also planned a kayak trip, which we rented. We prepared everything you needed, especially life jackets, drinks and food. We chose one island not too far from the shore. It was really breathtaking, we rowed with my wife and the children looked at the surrounding nature, especially at the fish that swam around our boat.

The island was covered mainly with sand, which is a rarity in this area because it is

exceptional. We anchored the boat
safely on the shore and got out. We
swam and dived, which was fantastic
because the water was so clear that
the visibility was several meters
deep. It was an experience we all
remember so far.

A few years ago, this island
was declared a protected area of
the highest degree, because
endangered species of birds nest
here. The island is no longer
accessible to the public, tourists
or fishermen.

And how it is today? Like
everything, this dam has changed.
It is no longer as clean as it was
years ago immediately after it was
refilled. The water as well as the
shores are polluted by rubbish
which were left here by people who
have nothing to do with nature.

Mountain stream and a small dam

We live in the north of our country where the weather during the summer used to be not as hot as in the south. But in recent years, everything has changed a lot and the temperature above +34°C in the summer is no longer anything special. Since all the swimming pools are too crowded during this period, we went with the children, who were still small to the nearby valley. We parked the car and went on a short trip to find a suitable place.

After a while, we found a suitable nook protected by trees and shrubs from the summer heat, where we have setthe blanket and prepared snacks, food and drink.

The mountain stream was very clean,
the children wore water shoes,
played in the water and were very
satisfied. With the help of stones,
I built a very small dam where they
could even sail on their tiny air
mattresses. Despite the fact that
it was a mountain stream, the water
was not cold, because it warmed up
sufficiently during these
exceptionally nice and sunny days.

When the summer was over, we
once went to this valley to see
what our place looks like. But we
couldn't find him at all. Our place
was no longer here, the way it
looked before. There was nothing
left of it at all.

Everything was destroyed.
Trees and shrubs around this place
were cut down, stones from the dam
scattered all around, burnt
remnants of wood were lying around

after the big fire, there was a lot
of dirt everywhere, rubbish and
grass was trampled. It was a really
repulsive look.
However, there was never anything
left of this magical place.

The Future world champions

The north of our country is
known not only for the mountains
but also for its lakes, dams and
ponds, which, when they freeze in
winter, their ice surface is a
source of rest, entertainment and
relaxation. I mean skating and
hockey.
That year we became world
champions in ice hockey. A tiny
state, but our boys gave a really
huge performance and we became
world champions in ice hockey. We
all rejoiced in it, we watched

every match and, of course, we kept
our fingers crossed for them.

We also like to go in winter,
if the weather allows and the water
surfaces freeze, out on the ice to
the ponds or lakes to look for
active rest and relaxation. We all
skate and we really like this
sport. Clean air, movement and,
above all, active rest.

That morning we went to the
nearest lake to skate. But on
arrival, we noticed a large number
of parked cars. There were a lot of
people everywhere and they were all
skating.
They were the youngest there barely
had several years accompanied by
their parents and grandparents, who
taught them to stand on skates.
There were also excellent skaters
who performed their pieces, whole
groups that played hockey and it

was really obvious that they are really good.

In short, on that day, a whole generation was on skates, and we saw that it was like our next natural movement, similar to walking or running.

That they would be other future successful champions? Who knows?

Mineral well

Our country is one of the smaller in terms of area, but the number and occurrence of mineral wells make us one of the leading countries in the world. The tradition has been known since ancient times and our world's most famous mineral baths with healing water were created in the Middle

Ages, which were visited by the
kings themselves.

In the north of our country
near the border, there are also a
number of mineral wells around
which the first known human
settlements originated in
prehistoric times.

We liked to visit one of such
wells together with children. They
were actually two iron vats into
which warm mineral water flowed
constantly from a large oven, so
the water was always clean.

There were often seen tourists
who stopped here after a
challenging hike, or cyclists who
arrived here, or in short, people
came here in cars to freshen.

People stopped here, undressed
in a bathing suit, took a short dip
in the water and rested, regardless
of whether it was snowing, freezing

or raining, or a strong wind was blowing. This water is really amazing for the regeneration of the body. In short, a natural open-air spa. We also often liked to refresh ourselves here this way.

Later, they built a small concrete tank a little higher up the valley towards the forest, into which, like these iron tanks, pure mineral water still flowed, and we also sometimes stopped here, especially in the summer. Today, this concrete reservoir is lowered and overgrown with grass. Water no longer flows into it.

After the next few years, they built a smaller recreational facility with two small pools in the place where the iron tubs, in which one of the two pools is hot water and the other is less warm. It is open-air, open all year round

and this small recreational
facility is still in use today and
is still very popular and
frequently visited.

But how everything is
constantly changing in the coming
years, right next to this small
recreational facility, which serves
to this day built an aqua park,
which has indoor and outdoor pools,
outdoor swimming pool, another pool
with artificial waves, wellness,
fitness, gym, restaurant, buffets,
accommodation and also built a ski
lift just a few meters from the
water park. But it is really very
well built, sensitively set in
nature and really at a very high
level of service.

We like to stop here after a
demanding hike or after a small
less than two and a half hour walk
in the vicinity.

Many times when we relax and
sunbathe outside in the mountain
sun we look at each other. But we
don't really have to say anything.
But with nostalgia, especially with
a smile, we remember the amazing
experiences in these parts, which
we experienced when swimming was
only in the original vats and in
the open air.

CONCLUSION

Every stay in nature bringing to us peace, relaxation, calm down and lot of energy. Don't underestimate the mountains and overestimate your strength. Please respect nature, protect our environment and don't pollute it.

Water, it is great source of energy without which we cannot be. And an icy crystal clear water is amazing experience with its stunning effect.

These stories do not always have a clear conclusion and explanation, I would like to leave this to the reader and his imagination.

I would like to take this opportunity to thank everyone who has contributed and supported my work in this way by purchasing this work. Many Thanks.

At the same time, I would like to thank my son who helped me with valuable advice and comments in editing this work and my wife for her support. Many Thanks.

THE STORIES II.

BY JAN KOMOROVSKY